YIN

YIN

NEW POEMS BY

CAROLYN KIZER

BOA EDITIONS, LTD.   BROCKPORT, NEW YORK · 1984

Grateful acknowledgment is made to the editors of publications in which many of the poems in this book, or earlier versions of them, first appeared:

American Review #16 (Bantam Books, Inc.): "Semele Recycled"; *American Review* #21 (Bantam Books, Inc.): "October, 1973"; *Antaeus*: "Fanny" and "Exodus"; *Choice*: "The Blessing," "Tu Foolery," and "Ancient Fathers"; *Grand Street*: "Cupid and Venus"; *Kayak*: "Running Away from Home," "Dangerous Games," "Race Relations," "Dream of a Large Lady," "Postcards from Rotterdam," "For My Daughter," and "For Sappho: After Sappho"; *The New Yorker*: "Dixit Insipiens" (originally entitled "The Unbelievers"); *Open Places*: "A Muse," "Threatening Letter," "Reading Your Poems," and "After Basho"; *Poetry*: "Afternoon Happiness," "Children," "Food of Love," and "Limbo"; *Saint Andrews Review*: "Medicine."

ISBN 0-918526-44-2 Cloth; 0-918526-45-0 Paper

Publications by BOA Editions, Ltd., a not-for-profit corporation under section 501 (c)(3) of the United States Internal Revenue Service Code, are made possible in part with the assistance of grants from the Literature Program of the New York State Council on the Arts and the Literature Program of the National Endowment for the Arts, a Federal Agency.

Designed and typeset at Visual Studies Workshop, Rochester, New York.

Distributed by Writers & Books, Inc., 892 South Clinton Street, Rochester, New York 14620

First Edition

BOA Editions, Ltd.
A. Poulin, Jr., President
92 Park Avenue
Brockport, New York 14420

To the memory of Ruthven Todd

CONTENTS

I

BELIEVING / UNBELIEVING

DIXIT INSIPIENS

At first, it was only a trickle
Of eminent men, with their astrolabes and armillae,
Who passed cautious notes to each other, obscurely worded.
Of course the terrible news leaked out
And the peasants were agitated.
Moans arose from the windowless hovels.
Men, hardly human, shouldering crude farm implements,
Gathered in knots along the roads and raved:
Storm the great houses! Smash the laboratory,
The retorts, the lenses — instruments of Satan.
But the minions of the manors
Lashed them back from the bronze gates,
Back to the foetid darkness, where they scoured their knees,
Praying for us.

The magnificent correspondence between Madame A.
And the more eminent, though less notorious,
Monsieur B. reveals a breathtaking indifference
To you: not even the target of a bilious epigram.
They move intently towards their prime concern:
Which voice, this time, will loose
Its thunderbolt? The straggling troops of revolution
Must be rallied yet again.
In perfect confidence of their powers,
As if they, who after all are people of flesh and bone,
Despite their attainments, had replaced you;
Not by storming the throne-room, nor by those manifestos
They so supremely compose.
You were swept out, and they swept in, that's all.

Out there, on the edge of the familiar world,
Are knots of men, burned dark as our own peasants
Used to be, but better armed, we know;
We armed them.
From time to time they bang their heads on the sand
And shout, unintelligibly, of you.
Their version of you, of course, quite different
From the blandness you metamorphosed into
Over the centuries, progressively edited.

Holy war! Can they be in earnest?
After all, this isn't the fourteenth century.
Is it the uneasiness we feel, or the remnants
Of ancestral superstition, which makes us ask ourselves,
Can this be your planned revenge?

How can you be vengeful when you don't exist?
If only the weight of centuries
Wasn't on your side.
If only unbelief was more like faith.

SEMELE RECYCLED

After you left me forever,
I was broken into pieces,
and all the pieces flung into the river.
Then the legs crawled ashore
and aimlessly wandered the dusty cow-track.
They became, for a while, a simple roadside shrine:
A tiny table set up between the thighs
held a dusty candle, weed, and fieldflower chains
placed reverently there by children and old women.
My knees were hung with tin triangular medals
to cure all forms of hysterical disease.

After I died forever in the river,
my torso floated, bloated in the stream,
catching on logs or stones among the eddies.
White water foamed around it, then dislodged it;
after a whirlwind trip, it bumped ashore.
A grizzled old man who scavenged along the banks
had already rescued my arms and put them by,
knowing everything has its uses, sooner or later.

When he found my torso, he called it his canoe,
and, using my arms as paddles,
he rowed me up and down the scummy river.
When catfish nibbled my fingers, he scooped them up
and blessed his re-usable bait.
Clumsy but serviceable, that canoe!
The trail of blood that was its wake
attracted the carp and eels, and the river turtle,
easily landed, dazed by my tasty red.

A young lad found my head among the rushes
and placed it on a dry stone.
He carefully combed my hair with a bit of shell
and set small offerings before it
which the birds and rats obligingly stole at night,
so it seemed I ate.
And the breeze wound through my mouth and empty sockets
so my lungs would sigh and my dead tongue mutter.

Attached to my throat like a sacred necklace
was a circlet of small snails.
Soon the villagers came to consult my oracular head
with its waterweed crown.
Seers found occupation, interpreting sighs,
and their papyrus rolls accumulated.

Meanwhile, young boys retrieved my eyes
they used for marbles in a simple game
—till somebody's pretty sister snatched at them
and set them, for luck, in her bridal diadem.
Poor girl! When her future groom caught sight of her,
all eyes, he crossed himself in horror,
and stumbled away in haste
through her dowered meadows.

What then of my heart and organs,
my sacred slit
which loved you best of all?
They were caught in a fisherman's net
and tossed at night into a pen for swine.
But they shone so by moonlight that the sows stampeded,
trampled each other in fear, to get away.
And the fisherman's wife, who had 13 living children
and was contemptuous of holy love,
raked the rest of me onto the compost heap.

Then in their various places and helpful functions,
the altar, oracle, offal, canoe, and oars
learned the wild rumor of your return.
The altar leapt up and ran to the canoe,
scattering candle grease and wilted grasses.
Arms sprang to their sockets, blind hands with nibbled nails
groped their way, aided by loud lamentation,
to the bed of the bride, snatched up those unlucky eyes
from her discarded veil and diadem,
and rammed them home. O what a bright day it was!
This empty body danced on the river bank.
Hollow, it called and searched among the fields
for those parts that steamed and simmered in the sun,
and never would have found them.

14

But then your great voice rang out under the skies
my name!—and all those private names
for the parts and places that had loved you best.
And they stirred in their nest of hay and dung.
The distraught old ladies chasing their lost altar,
and the seers pursuing my skull, their lost employment,
and the tumbling boys, who wanted the magic marbles,
and the runaway groom, and the fisherman's 13 children
set up such a clamor with their cries of "Miracle!"
that our two bodies met like a thunderclap
in mid-day—right at the corner of that wretched field
with its broken fenceposts and startled, skinny cattle.
We fell in a heap on the compost heap
and all our loving parts made love at once,
while the bystanders cheered and prayed and hid their eyes
and then went decently about their business.

And here it is, moonlight again; we've bathed in the river
and are sweet and wholesome once more.
We kneel side by side in the sand;
we worship each other in whispers.
But the inner parts remember fermenting hay,
the comfortable odor of dung, the animal incense,
and passion, its bloody labor,
its birth and rebirth and decay.

THE BLESSING

I.

Daughter-my-mother,
you have observed my worst.
Holding me together at your expense
has made you burn cool.

So did I in childhood:
nursed her old hurts and doubts,
myself made cool to shallowness.
She grew out as I grew in.
At mid-point, our furies met.

My mother's dust has rested
for fifteen years
in the front hall closet
because we couldn't bear to bury it.
Her dust-lined, dust-coated urn
squats among the size-eleven overshoes.
My father, who never forgets
his overshoes,
has forgotten that.

Hysterical-tongued daughter
of a dead marriage,
you shed hot tears in the bed
of that benign old woman
whose fierce joy you were:
tantrums in the closet
taking upon yourself the guilt
the split parents never felt.

Child and old woman
soothing each other,
sharing the same face
in a span of seventy years,
the same mother wit.

II.

I must go home, says my father,
his mind straying;
this is a hard time
for your mother. But she's been dead
these fifteen years.
Daughter and daughter, we sit
on either side.
Whose? Which? He's not sure.
After long silence,
don't press me, he says.

Mother, hysterical-tongued,
age and grace burned away
your excesses, left
that lavender-sweet child
who turned up the thermostat
on her electric blanket, folded
her hands on her breast.
You had dreamed death
as a silver prince:
like marrying Nehru, you said.

Dearest, does your dust hum
in the front hall closet—
this is a hard time for me—
among the umbrella points,
the canes, and overshoes
of that cold climate?

Each week she denies it,
my blithe mother
in that green, cloud-free landscape
where we whisper our dream-secrets
to each other.

III.

Daughter, you lived through
my difficult affairs

as I tried to console
your burnt-out childhood.
We coped with our fathers,
compared notes
on the old one and the cold one,
learned to moderate our hates.
Risible in suffering,
we grew up together.

Mother-my-daughter,
I have been blessed
on both sides of my life.
Forgive me if sometimes
like my fading father
I see you as one.

Not that I confuse
your two identities
as he does, taking off
or putting on his overshoes,
but my own role:

I lean on the bosom
of that double mother,
the ghost by night, the girl by day;
I between my
two mild furies,
alone but comforted.

And I will whisper blithely
in your dreams
when you are as old as I,
my hard time over.
Meanwhile, keep warm
your love, your bed,
and your wise heart and head,
my good daughter.

for Ashley

DANGEROUS GAMES

I fly a black kite on a long string.
As I reel it in,
I see it is a tame bat.
You say it's you.

You fly a white kite, but the string snaps.
As it flutters down,
You see it is a cabbage butterfly.
I say it's I.

You invented this game,
Its terms, its terminology.
I supplied the string,
Giving you the frayed length
So I could escape.

I flew a black kite, let go the string,
But the thing darted down
Straight for my long hair
To be entangled there.

You flew a white kite that ran away.
You chased it with your bat sonar.
But you found only a cabbage butterfly
Trembling on an aphid-riddled leaf.

THE COPULATING GODS

Brushing back the curls from your famous brow,
Lingering over the prominent temple vein
Purple as Aegean columns in the dawn,
Calm now, I ponder how self-consciously
The gods must fornicate.
It is that sense of unseen witness:
Those mortals with whom we couple or have coupled,
Clinging to our swan-suits, our bull-skins,
Our masquerades in coin and shrubbery.

We were their religion before they were born.
The spectacle of our carnality
Confused them into spiritual lust.
The headboard of our bed became their altar;
Rare nectar, shared, a common sacrament.
The wet drapery of our sheets, molded
To noble thighs, is made the basis
For a whole new aesthetic:
God is revealed as the first genius.

Men continue to invent our histories,
Deny our equal pleasure in each other.
Club-foot, nymphomanic, they dub us,
Then fabricate the net that God will cast
Over our raptures: we, trussed up like goats,
Paraded past the searchlights of the sky
By God himself, the ringmaster and cuckold,
Amidst a thunderous laughter and applause.

Tracing again the bones of your famous face,
I know we are not their history but our myth.
Heaven prevents time; and our astral raptures
Float bouyant in the universe. Come, kiss!
Come, swoon again, we who invented dying
And the whole alchemy of resurrection.
They will concoct a scripture explaining this.

20

CHILDREN

What good are children anyhow?
> They only break your heart.
The one that bore your fondest hopes
> will never amount to anything.
The one you slaved to give the chances you never had
> rejects them with contempt.
They won't take care of you in your old age.
> They don't even write home.
They don't follow in your footsteps.
They don't avoid your mistakes.
It's impossible to save them from pain.
> And of course they never listen.

Remember how you hung on the lips
> of your father or grandfather,
Begging for the old stories:
> "Again! Tell it again!
> What was it like 'in olden times'?"
We have good stories too:
> funny, instructive, pathetic.
Forget it. Write them down for your friends.
Your friends, with whom you have that unspoken pact:
Don't ask me about my children, and I won't inquire of yours.

Remember how we used to exchange infant pictures?
How we boasted of cute sayings? How we . . .
> Forget it.
Put away those scrapbooks, with the rusted flute in the closet,
> with the soiled ballet-slippers.
Tear up the clumsy Valentines.
Tear up every crayoned scrap that says, "I love you, Mama."
They don't want us to keep these mementoes:
> they find them embarrassing,
These relics of dependent love,
The orange crayon that didn't dare write, "I hate you."
Forget their birthdays, as they forget yours.

Perhaps because they never finish anything,
> not a book, not a school,

Their politics are cruel and sentimental:
Some monster of depravity
                    who destroyed millions with his smile,
Who shadowed our youth with terror,
                    is a hero to them.
Now he smiles benignly from their walls.

Because they are historyless, they don't believe in history:
                    Stalin wasn't so bad.
                    The Holocaust didn't really happen.
                    Roosevelt was a phony.
But the worst of it is:
                    they don't believe we ever believed;
They don't believe we ever had ideals.
They don't believe that we were ever poor.
They don't believe that we were passionate
                    —or that we are passionate today!
Forget it. Don't torture yourself.
                    You still have some life to salvage.
Get divorced. Go on a diet.
Take up the career you dropped for them twenty years ago.
Go back to the schools they deserted, and sign up for courses:
Study Tranquility 101; take Meditation; enroll for Renewal.

Remember those older friends we used to envy,
                    brilliant and glittering with beauty,
Who refused to have children,
                    not about to sacrifice their careers;
Who refused the mess, the entrapment,
                    as we toiled over chores and homework,
                    worried about measles and money—
Have you seen them lately?
They no longer converse in sparkling cadenzas.
They are obsessed with their little dog
                    who piddles on the Oriental rug,
                    who throws up on the bedspread.

22

They don't notice his bad breath;
His incessant yapping doesn't seem to disturb them.
To be honest about it,
                              the whole apartment smells!
And the way they babble to him in pet names
                              instead of talk of Milton, Chaucer, Dante.
The way they caress him makes you fairly ill;
                              the way they call him, "Baby."

IN THE FIRST STANZA,

first, I tell you who I am:
shadowed, reflective, small,
pool in an unknown glade.
It is easy to be a poet,
brim with transparent water.
In autumn, the leaves blow down
over the ruffled surface,
sink to rest, then resume their cycle.

In the second stanza, you laugh,
skipping pebbles across my surface
charmed by the spreading circles.
In the trees' perpetual twilight
you are alone with the poet.
Gently, you shake your head.
You know me as turbulent ocean
clouded with thunder and drama.

In the third stanza, I die.
Still, I insist on composing
as my throes go on and on.
I clench the pen in my teeth
making those furious scratches
that you will see, much later,
as a graceful calligraphy:
drift of sails that sketch my horizon.

My hands, in the fourth stanza,
with the agonized clutch of the dying,
draw your hand beneath the covers.
I beg you to travel my body
till you find the forest glade.
Then your hand, like a leaf in autumn,
is pulled into the pool.
The rest of you doesn't believe it.

The fifth stanza begins
with water, and quiet laughter.
Then I die, I really die.
You pick up this piece of paper.
You read it aloud and explain me,
my profile cast in prose.
It drops from your hand like a leaf.
This is all part of the cycle.

Then, in the final stanza,
I tell you who I am.

RACE RELATIONS

I sang in the sun
of my white oasis
as you broke stone

Then I sang and paraded
for the distant martyrs
loving the unknown

They lay still in the sun
of Sharpeville and Selma
while you broke stone

When you fled tyranny
face down in the street
signing stones with your blood

Far away I fell silent
in my white oasis
ringed with smoke and guns

Martyred in safety
I signed for lost causes
You bled on   You bled on

Now I recommence singing
in a tentative voice
loving the known

I sing in the sun
and storm of the world
to the breakers of stone

You are sentenced to life
in the guilt of freedom
in the prison of memory

Haunted by brothers
who still break stone
I am sentenced to wait

And our love-hate duet
is drowned by the drum
of the breakers of stone

for D.B.

FOOD OF LOVE

Eating is touch carried to the bitter end.
—Samuel Butler II

I'm going to murder you with love;
I'm going to suffocate you with embraces;
I'm going to hug you, bone by bone,
Till you're dead all over.
Then I will dine on your delectable marrow.

You will become my personal Sahara;
I'll sun myself in you, then with one swallow
Drain your remaining brackish well.
With my female blade I'll carve my name
In your most aspiring palm
Before I chop it down.
Then I'll inhale your last oasis whole.

But in the total desert you become
You'll see me stretch, horizon to horizon,
Opulent mirage!
Wisteria balconies dripping cyclamen.
Vistas ablaze with crystal, laced in gold.

So you will summon each dry grain of sand
And move towards me in undulating dunes
Till you arrive at sudden ultramarine:
A Mediterranean to stroke your dusty shores;
Obstinate verdure, creeping inland, fast renudes
Your barrens; succulents spring up everywhere,
Surprising life! And I will be that green.

When you are fed and watered, flourishing
With shoots entwining trellis, dome and spire,
Till you are resurrected field in bloom,
I will devour you, my natural food,
My host, my final supper on the earth,
And you'll begin to die again.

RUNNING AWAY FROM HOME

1.

Most people from Idaho are crazed rednecks
Grown stunted in ugly shadows of brick spires,
Corrupted by fat priests in puberty,
High from the dry altitudes of Catholic towns.

Spooked by plaster madonnas, switched by sadistic nuns,
Given sex instruction by dirty old men in skirts,
Recoiling from flesh-colored calendars, bloody gods,
Still we run off at the mouth, we keep on running.

Like those rattling roadsters with vomit-stained back seats,
Used condoms tucked beneath floor-mats,
That careened down hairpin turns through the blinding rain
Just in time to hit early mass in Coeur d'Alene!

Dear Phil, Dear Jack, Dear Tom, Dear Jim,
Whose car had a detachable steering-wheel;
He'd hand it to his scared, protesting girl,
Saying, "Okay *you* drive"—steering with his knees;

Jim drove Daddy's Buick over the railroad tracks,
Piss-drunk, just ahead of the Great Northern freight
Barrelling its way thru the dawn, straight for Spokane.
O the great times in Wallace & Kellogg, the good clean fun!

Dear Sally, Dear Beth, Dear Patsy, Dear Eileen,
Pale, faceless girls, my best friends at thirteen,
Knelt on cold stone, with chilblained knees, to pray,
"Dear God, Dear Christ! Don't let him go All The Way!"

O the black Cadillacs skidding around corners
With their freight of drunken Jesuit businessmen!
Beautiful daughters of lumber-kings avoided the giant
Nuptial Mass at St. Joseph's, and fled into nunneries.

The rest live at home; bad girls who survived abortions,
Used Protestant diaphrams, or refused the sacred obligation
Of the marriage bed, scolded by beat-off priests,
After five in five years, by Bill, or Dick, or Ted.

29

I know your secrets; you turn up drunk by 10 a.m.
At the Beauty Shoppe, kids sent breakfastless to school.
You knew that you were doomed by seventeen.
Why should your innocent daughters fare better than you?

Young, you live on in me; even the blessed dead:
Tom slammed into a fire hydrant on his Indian Chief
And died castrated; Jim, fool, fell 4 stories from the roof
Of his jock fraternity at Ag. & Tech.;

And the pure losers, cracked up in training planes
In Utah; or shot by a nervous rookie at Fort Lewis;
At least they cheated the white-coiffed ambulance chasers
And death-bed bedevillers, and died in war in peace.

          2.
Some people from Oregon are mad orphans
Who claim to hail from Stratford-upon-Sodom.
They speak fake B.B.C.; they are Unitarian fairies,
In the Yang group or the Yin group, no Middle Way.

Some stay Catholic junkies, incense sniffers who
Scrawl JESUS SAVES on urinal walls, between engagements;
Or white disciples of Black Muslims; balding blonds
Who shave their pubic hair, or heads, for Buddha.

I find you in second-hand bookstores or dirty movies,
Bent halos like fedoras, pulled well down,
Bogarts of buggery. We can't resist the furtive questions:
Are you a writer too? How did you get out?

We still carry those Rosary scars, more like a *herpes
Simplex* than a stigmata: give us a nice long fit
Of depression; give us a good bout of self-hate;
Give us enough Pope, we pun, and we'll hang.

Hung, well hung, or hungover, in the world's most durable
Morning after, we'd sooner keep the mote and loose the eye.
Move over, Tonio Kröger, you never attended
Our Lady of Sorrows, or Northwestern High!

30

Some people from Washington State are great poetasters,
Imbibers of anything, so long as it makes us sick
Enough to forget our sickness, and carry on
From the Carry Out: Hostess Winkies and Wild Duck.

We "relate," as they say, to Indians, bravest of cowards
Furtively cadging drinks with a shit-faced grin:
Outcasts who carry our past like a 90 lb. calcified foetus
We park in the bus-station locker, and run like sin.

Boozers and bounders, cracked-up crackerbarrel jockeys,
We frequent greasy bistros: Piraeus and Marseilles;
As we wait for our rip-off pimps, we scribble on napkins
Deathful verse we trust our executors to descry.

Wills. We are will-less. As we have breath, we are wilful
And wishful, trusting that Great Archangel who Still Cares,
Who presides at the table set up for celestial Bingo.
We try to focus our eyes and fill in the squares.

                        3.
Some people from Spokane are insane salesmen
Peddling encyclopedias from door to door,
Trying to earn enough to flee to the happy farm
Before they jump from the Bridge or murder Mom;

Or cut up their children with sanctified bread-knives
Screaming, "You are Isaac, and I am Abraham!"
But it's too late. They are the salutary failures
Who keep God from getting a swelled head.

Some shoot themselves in hotel rooms, after gazing
At chromos of the Scenic Route through the Cascades
Via Northern Pacific, or the old Milwaukee & St. Paul:
Those trains that won't stop rattling in our skulls!

First they construct crude crosses out of Band-Aids
And stick them to the mirror; then rip pages
From the Gideon Bible, roll that giant final joint,
A roach from *Revelations*, as they lie dying.

Bang! It's all over. Race through Purgatory,
At last unencumbered by desperate manuscripts
In the salesman's sample-case, along with the dirty shirts.
After Spokane, what horrors lurk in Hell?

4.

I think continually of those who are truly crazy:
Some people from Montana are put away;
They shake their manacles in a broken dance,
With eyes blue-rimmed as a Picasso clown's.

Still chaste, but nude, hands shield their organs
Like the original Mom & Dad, after the Fall;
Or they dabble brown frescoes on the walls
Of solitary: their Ajanta and Lascaux.

While the ones that got away display giant kidneys
At the spiral skating-rink of Frank L. Wright,
Or framed vermin in the flammable Museum
Of Modern Mart. But they're still Missoula

In their craft and sullen ebbing, Great Falls & Butte.
Meanwhile, Mondrian O'Leary squints at the light
Staining the white radiance of his well-barred cell,
Till ferocious blurs bump each other in Dodgem cars.

O that broken-down fun-house in Natatorium Park
Held the only fun the boy Mondrian ever knew!
Now seven-humped, mutated radioactive Chinook salmon
Taint the white radiance of O'Leary's brain.

O mad Medical Lake, I hear you have reformed;
No longer, Sunday afternoon, the tripper's joy.
Watch the nuts weep! or endlessly nibble fingers.
Funny, huh? The white ruin of muscular men

Twisting bars like Gargantua; lewd Carusos,
Maimed Chanticleers, running off at the scars.
They hoot their arias through the rhythmic clashing
Of garbage-can lids that serve as dinner trays;

Inmates are slopped, while fascinated on-
Lookers watch Mrs. Hurley, somebody's grandma,
Eating gravy with her bare hands. Just animals, Rosetta.
She's not *your* mother. Don't let it get you.

Suddenly, Mr. Vincente, who with his eleven brothers
Built roads through the Spokane Valley
Where Italians moved like dreams of Martha Graham
As they laid asphalt over subterranean rivers,

Spots a distant cousin, Leonard, an architect
Until seventh grade, who seems to know him:
Leonard displays, by way of greeting,
His only piece of personal adornment:

How the tourists squeal! Watch them fumble at coat, and fly!
Girdled and ginghamed relatives disperse
Back to the touring car, the picnic basket
With its home-made grappa in giraffe-necked bottles.

As sun-scarred men urge olive children on,
Grandma Hurley, who thought the treat was for her,
Shyly waves her gravy-dappled fingers,
Couple-colored as her old brindled cat.

Enough of this madness! It's already in the past.
Now they are stabbed full of sopers, numbed & lobotomized
In the privacy of their own heads. It's easier for the chaplain:
They're nodding. If you consent to be saved, just nod for God.

It's never over, old church of our claustrophobia!
Church of the barren towns, the vast unbearable sky,
Church of the Western plains, our first glimpse of brilliance,
Church of our innocent incense, there is no goodbye.

Church of the coloring-book, crude crayon of childhood,
Thank God at last you seem to be splitting apart.
But you live for at least as long as our maimed generation
Lives to curse your blessed plaster bleeding heart.

II

A MUSE

A MUSE

"The baby was wakened from her afternoon nap today by a fierce wind blowing up and rain. . . . She danced around a few times and came to me speaking with her little face close to me,

" 'When the wind blows in your eyes and makes a *turble* song in your ears, you *cry out*, and biz around like this,' and she was off on another little dance. She lacks four days of being two years and five months old today." That is my forty-seven-year-old mother speaking, of me, her first and only child. She is a woman "liberated" by necessity if not by choice. Losing her mother at thirteen (grandmother had just given birth to a son whose cleft palate split his face open from nose to chin: her sixth living child among a number of miscarriages and a baby, Little Will, lost at one and half from scarlet fever; "she just turned her face to the wall and died," mother said), she raised her younger brothers and took care of her father; earned a B.A. from Boulder and a doctorate from Stanford in biology, which she taught at Mills and San Francisco State; she lived a bohemian life in San Francisco while contributing most of her earnings to send three brothers through college; at some point (my chronology is somewhat shaky here, as all this information was conveyed orally, and in scraps) she studied art and philosophy at Harvard, with Dow and Santayana respectively; she ran the first federally sponsored drug clinic in New York city in a Rockefeller home that is now the site of the Museum of Modern Art, she was an organizer for the I.W.W. and assisted Anna Louise Strong on her paper, *The Union Record*, in Seattle during the terrible union-management-Pinkerton strife around 1918; and when she met my father in Spokane, in her mid-forties, she was working for the government, investigating the conditions of women in the mines and lumber camps of the Northwest. But now, all that energy, all that talent, all that passion, is focussed on maternity, on me.

I am already, from mother's evidence, a genius. The truth that nearly all children from the ages of around three to six are geniuses is something of which she has first-hand knowledge—brothers, social work, teaching kindergarten—but that information is carefully compartmentalized, kept from herself, and me.

You can see that I am rife with possibility; a dancer, yes, and it may be a choreographer, and a poet, a poet who dances to her own music, her own words. In the tradition of the revered Isadora.

A year and a half later, I am visiting "the San" with mother at

37

Christmas. "The San" is a charitable tuberculosis sanitarium that my grandfather runs for the State of California, assisted by two of my mother's brothers, one a doctor, one a ne'er-do-well with the thickened speech and the scarred and twisted lip of a crudely mended cleft palate. I *remember* the following scene for reasons that will become obvious:

Grandfather is in his easy chair, listening to the radio. Bob and Charles, my uncles, are painting a bookcase Chinese red. I smell the lacquer as I write these words. My mother is watching me intently as I mess around with a paper and crayons, struggling to form letters of the alphabet. Laboriously, I form the letters A, R, T, in what might generously be called a crooked line, and hold it up for mama's approval. Sensation. *Her first word!* In her wonderfully dramatic way, my mother announces that this proves my extraordinary gifts; further, it proves that I am *fated* to become an artist. Do I remember (see, hear, smell) this episode so vividly because I realize that at that moment my fate was sealed? I think not. I remember it because I was entirely aware at the time that the conjunction of the letters A, R, T, was wholly accidental. I believe that I tried to mumble something to that effect at the time, but of course nobody paid any attention. I remember the incident, friends, because I have suffered from a bad conscience ever since. I have never believed that I was what my mother (and thus everyone who was to follow) thought I was. Of course, nobody could have been. Do I blame my mother? No. Do I blame me? Don't we all?

In the scrapbook in which my mother carefully mounted every example of my burgeoning genius (and which I haven't quite had the heart to throw on the dump, much as I am tempted), we come across a "poem" composed when I was just five, which runs as follows:

> My breath runs in front me.
> I am running after it.
> I am catching my breath.

What this garden-variety bit of talent reveals is that I have been, almost from birth, irresistably drawn to the bad pun. Another example, twenty days later (yes, each of these *immortelles* is carefully dated): I am splashing and shouting in the tub. My father, as usual, tells me not to disturb him. I reply that, "I'm a wet Democrat, making a speech." ("Wet," O younger generation, was the label for an anti-Prohibitionist.) The Greeks exposed children like this on a hillside, especially girls, but I regret to say that I was positively encouraged along these lines, and tendencies developed that I have never quite been able to eradicate. Encouraged by my mother, that is. My father just wanted quiet, obedience, and a captive audience for him to read aloud to when his law practice didn't allow enough scope for his histrionic energies.

In retailing the excesses of a spoilt childhood, it is difficult to avoid irony, but from now on, I shall try: I'm not sure from any of the foregoing if you get the picture of my mother as a lovable woman. She was, intensely lovable, by virtue of her ambient charm, her looks (though tending to fat in her fifties, which I found comfy, and so did the men who came to dinner and who promptly fell for her, her style, and her cuisine), her considerable abilities as a raconteuse, and above all, her concern for the unfortunates of this world, a concern so unforced, sensitive, opulent in its man-ifestations that she was widely beloved by people who barely knew her. It is hard to leave out the thousand examples that illustrate these qualities, but I must cling to this chronicle of the "making" of a poet—for make me she did, in all senses, not excluding the sex-ual. I suppose the greatest testimony to her seductive lovableness is that I really forgive her for the unending overestimation and exploi-tation of my abilities, which drove me mad, and which I was pow-erless to abate.

The next stage was one of outings, picnics, and play-parties at home when, as well-equipped with the paraphernalia of creation, pen, pencils, paper, scissors, as any artist could have wished, I and she collaborated. So, in going through the infamous scrapbook, I am often puzzled to determine which was her contribution, which mine. As a general rule, if the end product looks suspiciously good, I suspect her fine and innocent Italian hand. During and after this period, I was beneficiary of lessons in every conceivable branch of the arts (except ballroom dancing, where my adamant refusal to be trapped in a long hall with unwilling members of the other sex was, for some reason, honored). What I really needed, from the cor-nucopia of my mother's own gifts, although I might have resisted at the time—being lazy, quick, and self-confident—was Latin and Greek, mother having had eight years of one and eleven of the other. The discipline would have been priceless, and the illumina-tion of my later life equally so. My mother's habitual self-denigra-tion seemed to poison for her the things at which she was truly bril-liant: languages, mathematics, bridge, the sciences. I was trained away from all of the above, and steered, God help me, toward "creativity." Creativity, the thing, above all, which life had denied her. I was to be fulfilled where she had been crippled. It didn't occur to me that what she was trying to create was a mirror-image of herself.

There was this capable, energetic, worldly woman, settled at last in marriage, to "a wonderful man," twenty-five years after her friends had given her up for lost, with a surprise baby that somehow crept in between marriage and menopause, and stuck—after years in San Francisco, Cambridge, New York, after befriending and being friended by artists, writers, radicals, the length and breadth of the land—in an archetypal small American town of the twenties. Why, I ask, was maternity enough for a woman who had done, and seen, and been, as much as she had? Why was I chosen to live the life she wanted, when she might well have gone on to live it herself? I can only surmise part of the answer. She had worked, worked, worked, largely for others, since the age of thirteen. Exceptionally sensitive and, beneath the charm and bravado, riddled with self-doubt, she had been dealt many a buffet by life, and many a low blow. She was tired. And, to herself, she was old. When I try to make sense of it, the cliché of a frail bird, battered by storms at sea, who finds safe haven, seems appropriate.

But why, after a few peaceful and probably boring years, when she had recovered her stamina, her nervous energy, did she not strike out again, and add a new career to the multifarious occupations of the past? My father wouldn't have opposed it. I think he would have welcomed it in fact, because he, too, had more of her neurotic concern showered upon him than he could have wanted. But he could, and did, escape to the office, into books (play quietly, now; your father's reading), leaving me to bear the brunt. Do I blame my father? You bet.

Most children, when told to "play quietly," know what to do, but I was sexually backward, so I wrote. I mean I really wrote, as distinct from saying things that my mother the amanuensis took down. Don't fear that I shall drag you through the scrapbook page by page, from the innocent effusions of infancy, through the assisted inspirations of childhood, to the eruptions of adolescence. Although it is tempting to prove that I made some advances from what you have read thus far, I am restrained by the awareness that until I reached the age of about twenty-nine (except for a couple of accidents we call "given" poems), I wrote nothing that would appeal to the adult mind, other than that of the authoress of my being.

Those early poems were written for her. They were given to her partly from love, partly as a bribe. The implicit barter: my poems, a partial invasion of my privacy, in exchange for some control over the rest of my life. Naive hope!

When I went to college, I managed to get as far away from Spokane, and her, as possible, short of wading into the Atlantic Ocean, pursued by her anxious, demanding biweekly letters. Enchanting letters, I discover now, when I come across them. Then they were read in a blur of guilt and tossed into the depths of my closet along with the unwashed laundry.

There, in the midst of many talented and well-educated girls, I discovered that I was less remarkable than I had been raised to believe. All those lessons in dancing, theatre, piano, singing, drawing, painting, modeling; the plays I had written and produced for my parents, Mrs. Anderson the laundress, and my playmates; the hand-made books, the poems by the dozen, the parodies, the serials, the songs—what did they prove? Not that I was in any way exceptional, but that my mother was.

Though I loved college, and studied with reasonable diligence, I dropped my "accomplishments" one by one. Painting and sculpting and drawing went first, and forever. Then the piano. Then singing. There was one last outburst: I wrote a sort of play, the music for it, choreographed it, and danced and acted in it, in collaboration with my college mates, and then retired from public life.

I published one poem in *The New Yorker*, then got a job dealing, among other things, with Indian labor statistics. I did not go back home except for short and infrequent vacations. Eventually I got married. I published one poem in *The Atlantic* and got pregnant again. I had three children in three years. I got divorced. My mother died. And then my serious life as a poet began. At last I could write, without pressure, without blackmail, without bargains, without the hot breath of her expectations.

I wrote the poems for her. I still do.

III

DREAMS AND FRIENDS

THE DYING GODDESS

The love goddess, alas, grows frailer.
She still has her devotees,
But their hearts are not whole.
They follow young boys
From the corners of their eyes.
They become embarrassed
By their residual myths.
Odd cults crop up, involving midgets,
Partial castration, dismemberment of children.
The goddess wrings her hands; they think it vanity,
And it is, partly.

Sometimes, in her precincts
Young men bow curly heads.
She sends them packing
Indulgently, with blown kisses.
There are those who pray endlessly,
Stretched full-length with their eyes shut,
Imploring her, "Mother!"
She taps her toe at these. A wise goddess
Knows her own children.

On occasion, her head raises
Almost expectantly: a man steps forward.
She takes one step forward,
They exchange wistful glances.
He is only passing.

When he comes to the place
Of no destination
He takes glass after glass
As her image wavers.
In her own mirror the image wavers.
She turns her face from the smokeless brazier.

DREAM OF A LARGE LADY

The large lady laboriously climbs
                    down the ladder from a gun emplacement.

She had gone up to contemplate
                    the blue view
                              and to damage the gun.

She has done neither
                    for the view was a baize haze
and the rooted gun immovable in stone.

                    So she climbs down the shaky ladder
                              with a few rungs missing
carrying her mostly uneaten
                    picnic lunch

of which she has consumed a single
                    hard-boiled egg
                              leaving the shell
not as litter but as symbolism
                    on the sullen gun
                              in its grey rotunda.

At the foot of the ladder she finds sand;
                    and one brown, shuttered house
from which another lady
                    stares.

This one wears a blurry face
                    and an orange dress
matching her orange hair
                    in a bun.

The large lady perforates along the beach
                    on her high-heeled pumps
                              by the water's verge,
as a large, pale water-bird might do.

When she reaches her own cottage
near the bay,
she finds a letter from the strange orange lady
in its crisp white envelope
lying on the table:

"I am an admirer of your poesy,
so I am baking you a fresh peach pie,"
the nice note reads.

"Do come to my house near the bay,"
she speaks in her head,
"Orange lady who admires my poesy.

"We will sit here quietly, in twilight,
and drink a cup of carefully brewed tea."

With a sigh, she puts aside the memory
of the grey gun she could only decorate
but not destroy.

Though clear in her eye she holds a vision:
the thin, ceremonious shell
of her eaten egg
painted by the sun against the sky.

READING YOUR POEMS IN YOUR HOUSE
WHILE YOU ARE AWAY

This morning my first roadrunner
paused on the dry wall you built
right outside your window.
A couple of playful jackrabbits
bounded among the cactus
under a chilly sun.

The mountains are mirage-like
as if they had just leaked
from one of your poems
and the god over there
had puffed them full of air
to float on a blur of sage
and desert broom.

Insubstantial mountains!
I found their serious weight
inside your books.
I found the serious roadrunner
not cartoon-like at all
with a tail full of adverbs.

I follow the dry wall
as it twists from page to page,
the glowing yellow stones
spontaneous but neat
nested together, held by your sweat;
rabbits, your cactus garden,
saguaro, living tombstones on the lawns,
dogs that serially howled at dawn,
your big white dog—when a coyote screamed.
And the bitter dark.

You remember I told you
after our night on the desert
I never see the first full moon
without thinking of you?

And your perfect poem about history:
How do you like nesting
in someone else's life?

Remember this when you come home:
One day, as you pause in composing,
a phrase of mine will leap into your stanza.
Just as, in writing this,
I borrow the words that belong to you
and give them back, like moonlight.

for Richard Shelton

THREE FROM TU FU

1.
TU FU to LI PO

My lord, how beautifully you write!
May I sleep with you tonight?
Till I flag, or when thou wilt,
We'll roll up drunken in one quilt.

In our poems, we forbear
To write of kleenex or long hair*
And how the one may fuck the other.
We're serious artists, aren't we, brother?

In our poems, oceans heave
Like our stomachs, when we leave
Late at night the fourteenth bar,
I, your meteor, you, my star.

When autumn comes, like thistledown,
We'll still be floating thru the town,
Wildly singing in the haze,
I, past saving, you, past praise.

*literally: fine paper and hair-pins, i.e., trivia

2.
MY HOME TOWN

When I go home, the old are older.
The aspens quiver, the winds blow colder.
I find that I am mildly celebrated:
My father, not my verse, is venerated.
And I fear daily that I shan't survive
This noble ancestor of ninety-five . . .

3.

FOR THE PRINCE IN EXILE
                (*Li Chin*, 750 A.D.)

Peerless and solitary
You allow me to stay
Our first meeting night:
The height of autumn,
The air crisp-clear.

                But the mists come soon,
                Then the rain,
                Then, towards morning,
                The milky moon.

                Then the thunder,
                Then the flood,
                Then your stoic sleep,
                While I drop tears
                You scorn to weep.

OCTOBER, 1973

Last night I dreamed I ran through the streets of New York
Looking for help for you, Nicanor.
But my few friends who are rich or influential
were temporarily absent from their penthouses or hotel suites.
They had gone to the opera, or flown for the weekend to Bermuda.
At last I found one or two of them at home,
preparing for social engagements,
absently smiling, as they tried on gown after gown
until heaps of rich, beautiful fabric were strewn
over the chairs and sofas. They posed before mirrors,
with their diamonds and trinkets and floor-length furs.
Smiling at me from the mirror, they vaguely promised help.
They became distracted—by constantly ringing phones,
by obsequious secretaries, bustling in with packages,
flowers, messages, all the paraphernalia,
all part of the uninterruptable rounds of the rich,
the nice rich, smiling soothingly, as they touched their hair
or picked up their phone extensions.
Absently patting my arm, they smiled, "It will be all right."

Dusk fell on the city as I ran, naked, weeping, into the streets.
I ran to the home of Barbara, my friend,
Who, as a young girl, rescued four Loyalist soldiers
from a Spanish prison;
in her teen-age sweater set and saddle shoes and knee socks,
she drove an old car sagging with Loyalist pamphlets
across the Pyrenees all the way to Paris without being caught.
And not long ago, she helped save a group of men
from Franco's sentence of death.

In my dream, Barbara telephones Barcelona.
I realize this isn't quite right,
but I just stand there paralyzed, as one does in dreams.
Then, dimly, from the other end of the line,
through the chatter of international operators,
we hear artillery fire, the faint tones of lost men,
cracked voices singing, "Los Quatros Generales"
                                    through the pulsations
of the great, twisted cable under the ocean.

Agonía, agonía, sueño, fermente y sueño.
Este es el mundo, amigo, agonía, agonía.

"No, Barbara!" I scream. "We are not back there.
That's the old revolution. Call up the new one."
Though I know that, every day,
your friends, Nicanor, telephone Santiago,
where the number rings and rings and rings
with never an answer. And now the rings
are turning into knells:

The church bells of Santiago
tolling the funeral of Neruda, his poems looted,
his autobiography stolen, his books desecrated
in his house on Isla Negra.
And among the smashed glass, the broken furniture,
his desk overturned, the ruined books strewn over the floor,
lie the great floral wreaths from the Swedish academy,
the wreaths from Paris, South Asia, the whole world over.
And the bells toll on . . .
Then I tell Barbara to hang up the phone.

She dials the number again, then turns to me, smiling,
smiling like an angel:
"He is there." "Trembling, I take the phone from her,
and hear your voice, Nicanor,
sad, humorous, infinitely disillusioned,
infinitely consoling:
"Dear Carolyn . . ." It *is* Nicanor!
And the connection is broken, because I wake up,
in this white room, in this white silence,
                                in this backwater of silence
on this Isla Blanca:
                        Nicanor, Nicanor,
are you, too, silent under the earth,
                        Brother? Brother?

54

MEDICINE

The practice of medicine
Is not what it was
In my grandfather's time.

I remember him telling me
Of weeks that went by
When he would be paid
Only in chickens
Or only potatoes;

Of treating the families
Of striking miners
In Montrose or Telluride
Who could not pay at all;
Of delivering babies
(A total of twenty)
For a tribe of dirt farmers
Who paid one new-laid egg
Or a cup of spring water:

After sweating a breach birth
And twins at that,
At five in the morning
It was mighty good water.

When, fifty years later
He came back to the mountains
Middle-aged babies
Ran up in the street
Crying, Doc! Doc! eyes streaming,
Tried to kiss his old hands.

No, the practice of medicine
Is not what it was,
But it has its moments:

That morning in surgery
I regained consciousness
A little too early
And found the doctor
Kissing my hand,
Whispering, whispering,
It's all right, darling,
You're going to live.

for W.S., MD

HOW IT PASSES

Tomorrow I'll begin to cook like mother:
All the dishes I love, which take her
Such hours to prepare:
The easy dishes that are so difficult
Like finnan haddie and beef stew
"That I wouldn't be ashamed to serve a king";
Her applesauce, bread pudding, lemon sponge,
All the sweet nursery foods
That prove I have a happy childhood.

Starting tomorrow, I'll be brave like father,
Now that I don't have those recurring nightmares
Of jackboots on the stairs, the splintered door
                                    just before dawn,
And the fascists dragging daddy out of bed,
Dragging him down the steps by his wonderful hair;
The screams as his spine cracks when he hits cement.
Then they make him brush his teeth with his own shit.
Though I know this is the price of bravery,
Of believing in justice and never telling lies,
And of being Benjamin, the best beloved.

I'll begin tomorrow. I'll learn how to work
Like my brilliant friends who speak in tongues,
Who drink and crack up, but keep on working,
While I waste my time in reading, reading, reading
The words of my brilliant and not-so-brilliant friends.
I promise to increase production, gather up
                                    all those beginnings
Of abandoned novels, whose insights astound me
As I contemplate their fading paragraphs.
I'll reveal how ambitious I have been in secret!

There is plenty of time.
I'll find the starter button soon.
After all, young women are meant to meander,
Bemused by fantasies of future loves.
It's just that I'm so sleepy tonight, so tired . . .
And when I wake up tomorrow, I'll be old.
And when night comes tomorrow,
It won't go away.

AFTER BASHO

Tentatively, you
slip onstage this evening,
pallid, famous moon.

THREATENING LETTER

I understand youre writing your autobiography youd better be careful remember Im a published author & can strike back I can get printed here for example & you cant anyway the children tell me I dont figure in it they dont either but if you omit your wife & children what can you possibly have to say of any interest nothing absolutely nothing has happened to you except us.

I suppose you will use the excuse i am writing this for my children even though they dont figure in it you will have chapter headings such as my reading in which you will discuss montaigne & stendahl no poetry philosophy or fiction since 1940 you said once i formed all my ideas in school now i dont have to think about them any more its just confusing & deflects me from my purpose that was one of the moments when I realized I have married a nut.

Other chapters will deal with your interest in politics & outdoor sports the latter including your career as a middleweight in college to falling off a mountain at age fifty-nine really at your age no one can say you've been inconsistent Ill bet you still carry that wornout clipping of kiplings if in your wallet.

The unifying principle behind all this is pain if it hurts it must be good for you everything from getting your teeth knocked out at twenty to freezing your balls at 12000 feet I have a great title for you mr negative incapability why not call it my non-life.

Just remember dont go back & put in anything about me I have refrained from writing about you for twenty years mainly from boredom but also because of our years together have faded like an old codachrome in sunlight remember me in the blue bikini on the bear rug with the baby you stretched out at my feet but if you should want to get nasty I feel sure I could resurrect some details & where memory fails invent so just hold down the old paranoia which would contaminate everything you said anyway & keep on including me out & I promise to ignore you when I write mine.

CUPID AND VENUS

*translated from the Scots
of Mark Alexander Boyd
(1563–1601)*

From bar to bar, from curb to curb I run,
From greasy alley walls I ricochet,
Blown over by my feeble fantasies
Till I drop like a roach from the linoleum.

Two gods guide me: one with a white cane,
Yes, he's a kid brought up to be a bum;
The gutter spawned the other one, a dame
Who roars like a rhino as she comes and comes.

A man pursues unhappiness forever,
Spewing out poems to drunks in the saloon,
And jacking off in the men's room in between.
But it's twice as bad to fool yourself that love
Leads anywhere: chasing that mad cunt up the stairs
As the kid, her blind pimp, eggs me on.

ANTIQUE FATHER

there is something
              you want urgently
                          to communicate
                                    to me

it is in your eyes
              of ancient
                          glacier water

I wait
              I try to listen
                          try to tolerate
your terrible silence

                          speak   Father

I believe you believe
              I am ready

                          we are both tense

I with expectancy
              and the terror you once
                          inspired in me

quelling all queries
              of my childhood

not the terror with which we
              (I over your shoulder)
                          gaze into the pit
eternity

                          Father speak
from the last edge
              where all folly
                          become wisdom
becomes folly again

                self-quelled   I listen
                            but the lesson
is your nervous silence
                        alone on the edge
more than you want to tell
                            you don't want
                                    to tell
your grave secret

                stern and reticent
                        you cannot say
that I cannot know

                    now will never know
                        if you ever knew

IV

FANNY AND THE AFFECTIONS

FANNY

At Samoa, hardly unpacked, I commenced planting.
When I'd opened the chicken crates, built the Cochins a coop.
The Reverend Mr. Claxton called, found me covered with mud,
My clothes torn, my hair in a wad, my bare feet bleeding.
I had started the buffalo grass in the new-made clearing.
The next day the priest paid a visit. Civil but restless,
I was dying to plant the alfalfa seed—gave him a packet.

That evening I paced up and down, dropping melon seeds,
Tomatoes and bush lima beans here and there
Where I thought they would grow. We were short of food now,
So I cooked up a mess of fat little parrots, disturbed
At the way they suggested cages and swings and stands. . .
An excellent meal. I have been told the dodo survived here,
And yearn for a pet on a string. I built the pig-house.

I had brought sweet coconut seed from Savage Island.
I planted kidney potatoes in small earthen hills.
Sowed seeds of eggplant in numerous boxes of soil,
Tomato and artichoke too; half-a-dozen fine pineapple
Sent over by Mr. Carruthers, the island solicitor.
As fast as we eat them, we plant the tops.
The kitchen a shack near the house. I made bread in the rain.

October, 1890. I have been here nearly a month;
Put in corn, peas, onions, radishes, lettuce. Lima beans
Are already coming up. The ripening cantaloupe were stolen.
Carruthers gave me mint root and grenadilla
Like a bouquet; he delivered a load of trees,
Two mangoes among them. I set them out in a heavy rain,
Then rounded off the afternoon sowing Indian corn.

Louis has called me a peasant. How I brooded!
Confided it to you, diary, then crossed it out.
Peasant because I delve in the earth, the earth I own.
Confiding my seed and root—I too a creator?
My heart melts over a bed of young peas. A blossom
On the rose tree is like a poem by my son.
My hurt healed by its cause, I go on planting.

No one else works much. The natives take it easy;
The colonials keep their shops, and a shortage of customers.
The mail comes four times a month, and the gossip all day.
The bars are crowded with amateur politicians,
Office-seekers I named the earwig counsul and king:
Big talkers, with small-time conspirators drinking them in.
Mr. Carruthers and I picked a site for the kitchen garden.

I was planting a new lot of corn and pumpkin
When a young chief arrived, laden with pineapple plants.
I set them out as I talked to him on the way home.
Rats and a wild hen ate the corn. Lettuce got too much sun.
So I dug a new patch up the road; in the fragrant evening
I confided to Louis, a puff of the sweetest scent
Blows back as I cast away a handful of so-called weeds!

It still hurts, his remark that I have the soul of a peasant.
My vanity, like a newly-felled tree, lies prone and bleeding.
I clear the weeds near the house for planting maize.
Sweet corn and peas are showing. I send for more seeds.
I clean out the potatoes, which had rotted in their hills.
Of course, RLS is not idle; he is writing A *Footnote to History:*
How the great powers combine to carve up these islands.

I discovered the ylang-ylang tree: a base for perfume,
Though it suggested to me the odor of boots.
Another tree is scented like pepper and spice,
And one terrible tree, I am forced to say,
Smells like ordure . . . It nearly made me ill.
Breadfruit is plentiful. I found a banana grove,
Began clearing it instantly, and worked till I was dizzy.

The garden looks like a graveyard: beds shaped like tombs.
I plant cabbage which I loathe, so the British won't tease me
For not growing it. But behold! in the hedge
Among citron and lime, many lemon trees, in full bearing.
Still, I will fall to brooding before the mirror,
Though Louis says he finds the peasant class "interesting."
He is forty today. I am ten years his senior.

On the cleared land, the green mummy-apple,
Male and female, is springing up everywhere.
I discover wild ginger, tumeric, something like sugar.
Roots of orange, breadfruit and mango, seeds of cacao
Came with a shipment from Sydney; also eleven
Young navel orange trees. The strawberry plants are rotten.
I am given a handful of bees. I plant more pineapple.

All fall I am cursed with asthma, rheumatics, a painful ear.
Christmas. A hurricane. And the New Year begins.
Louis describes it divinely to Henry James.
Mr. Carruthers' gift pineapple starts to fruit.
I set out one precious rhubarb plant, pause to gloat
At the ripe tomatoes, the flourishing long-podded beans.
But the neighbors' horses break in and trample the corn.

Sometimes, when planting, a strange subterranean rumble
—Volcanic?—vexes the earth beneath this peasant haunch.
I rise up from my furrow, knuckle smooth my brow
As I sniff the air, suddenly chemical, a sulphurous fume.
Louis insisted on going to Sydney, fell ill again.
His mother comes back with him, finds me on my knees.
The old lady's heart leaps! Alas, I am planting, not praying.

We both rise at five thirty, after dreaming of weeds,
Louis describes to me endless vivid deeps:
Dreams of nettle-stings, stabs from the citron's thorns,
The ants' fiery bites, the resistance of mud and slime,
The evasions of wormy roots, the dead weight of heat
In the sudden puffs of air . . . Louis writes till nine,
Then if he's well enough, he helps with the weeding.

He writes Colvin, keeper of prints at the British Museum,
"I know pleasure still . . . with a thousand faces,
None perfect, a thousand tongues, all broken,
A thousand hands, all with scratching nails . . .
High among joys, I place this delight of weeding,
Out here alone by the garrulous water, under the silence
Of the high wind, broken by sounds of birds."

The shock of bird-calls, laughing and whistling!
They mimic his name till it seems, he says,
"The birds relive the business of my day."
But the rains continue to fall on birds and weeds.
The new servants fooled around with the ice machine
As the house leaked and listed. Mildew spread its failure.
Mrs. S. gave me some nuts, and went back to Australia.

Green peppers, eggplant, tomatoes are flourishing,
Asparagus also. The celery does to season soup.
Avocadoes grow at a rate that is almost frightening.
Coconuts too. I read about Stanley and Livingstone.
I cured my five ulcers with calomel, wished I could tell
Stanley the remedy. Instead, I made perfume.
The servants feared devils, so I planted the orange grove alone.

For two months I misplaced this diary . . .
War is in the air, talk of killing all whites.
I bought coffee trees, rose trees and Indian beans,
Then went to Fiji to rest, and to get more seeds
From a former Kew gardener. An Indian in a shop
Told me how to raise Persian melon and cauliflower
And a radish that turns into a turnip when it grows up.

I came home to a burgeoning world: cacao, custard squash.
The new house was finished, and painted peacock blue.
The jealous old cat bit off the new cat's toes.
My mother-in-law returned with her Bible and lady's maid;
My daughter, her family, and my son Lloyd came too.
The relatives had a terrible row. Mrs. S. refused
To pray with the servants. I throw up my hands!

My diary entries grow farther and farther apart.
I wrote life was a strain. Later, someone crossed it out.
In pain again, from an aneurysm inside my head . . .
I planted more and more cacao, and a form of cherry tree,
Tobacco and rubber, taught how by Mr. Sketchley.
I planted more cacao through an epidemic of 'flu.
Three hundred seeds in baskets broke through the ground.

I get almost no time to write. I have been planting . . .
Four kinds of cabbage are doing very well.
Mr. Haggard, the land commissioner, come to dine,
Points out a weed which makes excellent eating
Cooked like asparagus. I shall try it very soon.
Now, when the Reverend Mr. Claxton comes to call,
I refuse to see him. I am tired of the Claxtons.

The political situation grows grim. I rage at Louis
Who toasts, "Her Blessed Majesty the Queen," then aggressively
Throbbing, turns to my American son
To say he may drink to the President *afterwards*
If he likes. I am writing this down
Hoping Louis will see it later, and be ashamed
Of his childishness and bad taste. (This will be erased.)

Because war is near, the Germans stop growing cacao.
Captain Hufnagel offers me all the seeds I can use.
So now we are blazing with cacao fever,
The whole family infected. Six hundred plants set out!
The verandah tracked with mud, and the cacao litter.
Mrs. S. upset by the mess. Twelve hundred cacaos planted.
Joe, my son-in-law, planted his thousandth tree today.

The tree onions make large bulbs but don't want to seed.
Most vigorous: sunflower, watermelon—weeds!
The jelly from berries out of the bush is delicious;
Lovely perfume from massoi, citron, vanilla and gum.
The peanuts are weeded while Joe plays on his flute.
I plant cabbage by moonlight, set out more cacao.
The heart of a death's-head moth beats a tattoo in my hand.

Planted coffee all day, and breadfruit, five beauties . . .
Planted coffee the better part of the day, eight plants.
In the nursery, three times that many. Planted coffee . . .
Painted the storm shutters. Planted coffee all morning.
I found a heap of old bones in a bush near the sty;
Two heads and a body: a warrior died with his prize.
Louis gave the bones a funeral and a burial.

A series of hurricanes. Louis writes to *The Times*
Of "the foul colonial politics." I send to New York for seeds:
Southern Cross cabbage, eggplant, sweet potato
And two thousand custard apples. Louis' own seed,
David Balfour, is growing. I wrote nothing
From June till the end of this year; too busy planting.
The Samoan princes are getting nearer to war.

It pains me to write this: my son-in-law has gone native
In a spectacular way. Belle is divorcing him.
Austin, my grandson, is in school in Monterey.
I have not, I believe, mentioned Mrs. Stevenson recently.
She has gone back to Scotland. The first breadfruit bore.
Belle and I go on sketching expeditions
To the hostile Samoan camps, stop in town for ginger beer.

Mr. Haggard begged us to stay in town
Because he bitterly wanted women to protect.
I suggested to him that I and my daughter
Could hide under his table and hand him cartridges
At the window, to complete the romantic effect.
It is clear that Mr. Haggard is Ryder's brother!
He said, "You'd sell your life for a bunch of banana trees."

I've given permission to most of the "boys"
To go to the races. Lloyd has put up the lawn tennis things.
Mr. Gurr, the neighbor, rushes in to say war has begun.
We all race to the mission. Eleven heads have been taken.
Later: Mr. Dine's cousin received a head smeared with black
(The custom is to return them to the bereaved).
He washed it off and discovered it was his brother.

He sat there, holding his brother's head in his hands,
Kissing it, bathing it with tears. A scandal arose
Because the heads of three girls have been taken as well
(Unheard of before in Samoa), returned wrapped in silk to their kin.

At Maile, the warriors danced a head-hunter's pantomime;
The men who had taken heads carried great lumps of raw pork
Between their teeth, cut in the semblance of heads.

72

I stopped writing this. Too hysterical with migraine.
Also, people find where I hide it, and strike things out.
Our favorite chief is exiled for life. The war winds down.
Louis works on his masterpiece, *The Weir of Hermiston*.
Well, I've kept him alive for eight more years,
While his dear friends would have condemned him to fog and rain
So they might enjoy his glorious talk in London,

Though it be the end of him. Fine friends! except for James.
Later: At six, Louis helped with the mayonnaise,
When he put both hands to his head, said, "Oh, what a pain!
Do I look strange?" I said no, not wanting to frighten him.
He was never conscious again. In two hours he died.
Tonight, the chiefs with their axes are digging a path
To the top of the mountain. They will dig his grave.

I will leave here as soon as I can, and never return,
Except to be buried beside him. I will live like a gipsy
In my wild, ragged clothes, until I am old, old.
I will have pretty gardens wherever I am,
But never breadfruit, custard apples, grenadilla, cacao,
Pineapple, ylang-ylang, citron, mango, cacao,
Never again succumb to the fever of planting.

POSTCARDS FROM ROTTERDAM

1.
Came such a long way
To find you—
Now only a channel
Separates us.
It is enough.

We are divided by water
I shed one tear.

2.
Waited for your letter
Until I lost interest.
Then it arrived,
Full of protestations.

Ah no, friend, you woo us with words
Just once.
Then you must lay your body
On the line.
And it isn't here.

3.
I thought
When the moon was full again
I would be in your arms.

But I'm not.

I'm in somebody else's arms.
We don't even glance
At the moon.

4.
Having wonderful time
Coming in from the town.

Having wonderful time
Contemplating the bidet.

Having wonderful time
With the shutters drawn.

Having wonderful time
Converting silver into dross.

Having wonderful time walking around
With a five-pound key in my purse

And a plastic flask full of Holland gin.
I shed one tear.

Wish you were here.
Love,
                Carolyn.

FOR MY DAUGHTER

Ashley's 25th Birthday

It was lingering summer
when you announced your birth.
As you were rapt in me,
rapt in a field-flower haze
of those last, listless days,
the waters burst
in a summer storm:
like Beethoven
your bold overture began.

It was sterile winter
in the birth-room zoo;
animals clung to the bars,
humped and yelled
as the fogs blew
through our primate skulls.
From a far distant self
I dreamily overheard
the worst, visceral howl.

Eyes opened to autumn
overnight: the trees
red against blazing blue
framed by a lutheran wall.
You were brought in to me
so pitiably small
and unbelievably red
as if god had dyed
the leaves and you
with the same mercurochrome.

Your young new parents,
terrified,
held on to one another
as they cried.
Later, your father
returned, with a stern smile,
handed me gold chrysanthemums
wrapt in damp newspaper
smelling of earth and death
and man-inflicted pain.
I held my breath that night
to the light sound of rain
and prayed you to grow.

From that time, you took
each season in your stride.
Still, when an ideal passion
for man or justice seizes
your fierce imagination
that birth-day glow is kindled
on your cheek and brow.

Now, as you have reached
your quarter-century,
with that same pristine fear
and undiminished pride
I thank your star, and you.

FOR SAPPHO: AFTER SAPPHO

1.

and you sang eloquently
for my pleasure
before I knew
you were girl or boy

        at the moment
        dawn awoke me
        you were in my bed

not sister   not lover
fierce though you were
a small cat
with thorny claws

        any daughter
        seeking comfort

you asked what you could give
to one who you thought
possessed everything

        then you forgot giving
        and tried to take
        blindly seeking the breast

what to do but hold you
lost innocent . . .

        we love whatever
        caresses us
        in need or pleasure
        a debt a favor
        a desperation

you were already
a speaking instrument
I loved the speaker
loved the voice
as it broke my heart with pity

        breath immortal
        the words nothing
        articulate poems
        not pertinent   the breath
        everything

you the green shoot
I the ripe earth
not yours to possess
alas   not yours

      2.
the punch bowl was full
a boy flirted
in our drunken dance
you dripped sweat
trembling shook your body
you tried to kill him
black darts shot from your eyes

        and the company laughed
        at your desperation

someone took you away
you lay on the grass
retching   then spewed your love
over the bed of crocus buds

        we led you home
        where I confronted
        your mother's picture
        my face enamelled

I have a slender daughter
a golden flower
your eyes are dark as olive pits
not for me to devour
child   no child of mine

        you screamed after me
        Aphrodite!   not giving
        as with a sweep of my cloak
        I fled skyward . . .

the full moon is shining
in the spring twilight
your face more pallid
than dry grass
and vomit-stained
still   you are the evening star

        most beautiful star
        you will die a virgin

Aphrodite thick-armed and middle-aged
loving the love of men
yet mourns you

        3.
        when I lost you
        where did you go
        only the fragments of your poems
        mourn you as I mourn you

and the unwritten poems lept with you
over the cliff-side

        hyacinth hair   rising
        in the rush of wind

hyacinth shattered
a dark stain on the ground
yet wine   some drops

80

some essence
has been distilled

       this mouth drinks thirstily
       as it chokes on the dust of your death

        4.
       yet I hold you in mid-air
       androgynous child of dream
       off-shoot of muses

my thought holds you
straight-browed and piercing-eyed
breastless as a boy
as light of foot

       wandering in that world
       beyond this   and before

but for now you forget it all
in Lethe
I too am treacherous   I forget everything
mind and limbs loosen
in the arms of a stranger
searching for Lethe

       but you dart through the future
       which is memory
       your boy's voice shouting out
       the remainder of poems
       of which I know
       simply beginnings

words heard a thousand times
in the echoing night
across the sea-foam

       separating us
       for this moment only

          in memoriam: S.L.M.B.

AFTERNOON HAPPINESS

At a party I spy a handsome psychiatrist,
And wish, as we all do, to get her advice for free.
Doctor, I'll say, I'm supposed to be a poet.
All life's awfulness has been grist to me.
We learn that happiness is a Chinese meal,
While sorrow is a nourishment forever.
My new environment is California Dreamer.
I'm fearful I'm forgetting how to brood.
And, Doctor, another thing has got me worried:
I'm not drinking as much as I should . . .

At home, I want to write a happy poem
On love, or a love poem of happiness.
But they won't do, the tensions of everyday,
The rub, the minor abrasions of any two
Who share one space. Ah, there's no substitute for tragedy!
But in this chapter, tragedy belongs
To that other life, the old life before *us*.
Here is my aphorism of the day:
Happy people are monogamous,
Even in California. So how does the poem play

Without the paraphernalia of betrayal and loss?
I don't have a jealous eye or fear
And neither do you. In truth, I'm fond
Of your ex-mate, whom I name, "my wife-in-law."
My former husband, that old disaster, is now just funny,
So laugh we do, in what Cyril Connolly
Has called the endless, nocturnal conversation
Of marriage. Which may be the best part.
Darling, must I love you in light verse
Without the tribute of profoundest art?

Of course it won't last. You will break my heart
Or I yours, by dying. I could weep over that.
But now it seems forced, here in these heaven hills,
The mourning doves mourning, the squirrels mating,
My old cat warm in my lap, here on our terrace

82

As from below comes a musical cursing
As you mend my favorite plate. Later of course
I could pick a fight; there is always material in that.
But we don't come from fighting people, those
Who scream out red-hot iambs in their hate.

No, love, the heavy poem will have to come
From *temps perdu*, fertile with pain, or perhaps
Detonated by terrors far beyond this place
Where the world rends itself, and its tainted waters
Rise in the east to erode our safety here.
Much as I want to gather a lifetime thrift
And craft, my cunning skills tied in a knot for you,
There is only this useless happiness as gift.

EXODUS

We are coming down the pike,
All of us, in no particular order,
Not grouped by age, Wanda and Val, her fourth husband,
Sallie Swift, the fellows who play bridge
Every Thursday, at Mason's Grill, in the back,
Two of them named George,
We are all coming down the pike.

Somebody whose face I can't make out
Is carrying old Mrs. Sandow, wrapped in a pink afghan;
Her little pink toes peep out from the hem
Of her cotton nightie like pink pea pods,
As pink as her little old scalp showing through.
Be careful, Mister, don't lose ahold of her.
She has to come down the pike.

Maybelle and Ruth walk together, holding hands;
Maybelle wears tennis shorts and a sweat-band
As she strides along steadily in her golf-shoes;
Ruth has on something flimsy,
Already ripped, and sling-backs, for God's sake.
But right now they are both coming down the pike.

Richard had to leave his piano; he looks sort of unfinished;
His long pale fingers wave like anemone
Or is it amoeba I mean?
He's artistic, but would never have been
Of the first rank, though he's changed his name three times.
He doesn't like the mob he's with,
But you can't be picky
When you're coming down the pike.

One of the monitors wants us to move faster,
But you can't really organize this crowd.
The latch on the bird-cage was loose so the budgie escaped
About two miles back, but Mrs. Rappaport still lugs his cage:
She's expecting the budgie to catch up any minute.
Its name was Sweetie. I can't stand pet names
And sentimentality at a time like this
When we should be concentrating all our efforts
On getting down the pike.

84

Who would have thought we would all be walking,
Except of course for Mrs. Sandow, and Dolly Bliss
In her motorized wheel-chair and her up-swept hair-do.
Someone has piled six hat-boxes on her lap;
She can hardly see over, poor lady, it isn't fair,
And who needs picture hats at a time like this.
But they are probably full of other things,
The kind of useless stuff you grab up in a panic
When there's no time to think or plan,
And you've got ten minutes before they order you down the pike.

Bill Watkins is sore that he wasn't chosen monitor
Because he lacks leadership qualities.
But he rushes up and down the lines anyhow
And snaps like a sheep-dog. The Ruddy family,
All eight of them red-heads, has dropped out for a picnic,
Using a burnt-out car
As a table. Not me, I'm saving my sandwiches.
The Ruddys were always feckless; they won't laugh tomorrow
When they run out of food on the pike.

Of course Al Fitch has nothing, not even a pocket-knife
Let alone a gun.
He had to get Morrie Phelps to shoot his dog for him.
No pets! You can see the reason for that,
Although nobody fussed about the budgie.
I expect there's a few smuggled cats
Inside some of the children's jackets.
But old Al Fitch, he just strolls along
With his hands in his pockets, whistling, "Goodnight Irene."

My husband says I shouldn't waste my breath
Describing us, but save it for the hike
Ahead; we're just like people anywhere
Though we may act crazier right now.
Maybelle drags Ruth along faster and faster
Though she's stumbling and sobbing, and has already fallen twice.
Richard, who's been so careful of his hands,
Just hit Al, and told him to whistle something else
Like Bach: one of the hymns he wrote, that we could sing.
Will you be trying to sing, wherever you are,
As you come down the pike?

ABOUT THE AUTHOR

Carolyn Kizer was born and raised in Spokane, Washington. After graduating from Sarah Lawrence College, she was a Fellow of the Chinese Government in Comparative Literature at Columbia University and subsequently lived in Nationalist China for one year.

In 1959 Carolyn Kizer founded the poetry journal, *Poetry Northwest*, which she edited until 1965; in 1964-1965 she was a Specialist in Literature for the United States Department of State in Pakistan; and from 1966 to 1970 she served as the first Director of the Literature Program for the newly created National Endowment for the Arts.

Since 1970 Carolyn Kizer has been Poet-in-Residence and Visiting Professor of Poetry in a variety of universities, including: the University of North Carolina at Chapel Hill, Columbia University, Ohio University, Washington University, the University of Iowa, the University of Maryland, the University of Cincinnati, the University of Louisville, and Bucknell University. She also has lectured and given readings of her poetry at numerous other colleges and universities throughout the United States and Europe.

Carolyn Kizer's previous books of poetry include *The Ungrateful Garden* (1961), *Knock Upon Silence* (1965), and *Midnight Was My Cry: New and Selected Poems* (1971). Ms. Kizer currently resides in Berkeley, California, with her spouse, John Marshall Woodbridge.

Yin has been issued in a first edition of three thousand copies, of which one thousand nine hundred and sixty are in paper and one thousand are in cloth. An additional forty copies have been specially bound by Gene Eckert in quarter-cloth and French papers over boards: twenty-five copies, numbered I–XXV and signed, also include a poem in holograph by Carolyn Kizer; fifteen copies, numbered i-xv and signed by Carolyn Kizer, have been retained by the publisher for presentation purposes.